Shojo Beat

Tail of the Moon

14

Story & Art by

Rinko Ueda

Volume 14

CONTENTS

Story Thus Far...

It is the Era of the Warring States. Usagi finally becomes a qualified ninja and marries Hanzo. But on the night of the wedding, Oda Nobunaga's army attacks their village! After leading Usagi to safety, Hanzo heads back to face the army. A few days later, Usagi returns to the village and is shocked to find Iga destroyed. She also hears that Hanzo is dead.

One year later, Usagi is working under Tokugawa Ieyasu at Okazaki Castle. She goes to Iga with her friend Yukimaru to investigate a rumor and is reunited with her great-grandpa, grandpa, and Goemon. Usagi then decides to marry Yukimaru when he tells her of his feelings for her.

Later, Usagi visits the capital and is abducted by Ranmaru. But just as she is about to be killed, a mysterious ninja saves her and returns her to Yukimaru. Usagi believes that it was Yukimaru who saved her. Unable to tell her the truth, Yukimaru suddenly kisses her!

Tail of the Moon

Chapter 92

ZZ
...!!

WHUP
OW...
MY MOUTH...
IT STILL HURTS...
I'M SO SORRY!!

THE MOMENT YUKI'S LIPS TOUCHED ME...
...I KNEW WITHOUT A DOUBT...

"NO."

"HE ISN'T THE ONE..."

AZUCHI CASTLE TOWN
EVER SINCE LORD NOBUNAGA BUILT THIS CASTLE IN AZUCHI, THERE HASN'T BEEN A SINGLE FIRE, YOU KNOW!!
NOBUNAGA'S RETAINER SADANARI MURAI
I'M SORRY...
RAN-MARU.
I HEARD THAT ON THE NIGHT OF THE FIRE, YOU WERE WITH THAT KUNOICHI YOU CAUGHT.
PERHAPS THE NINJA WHO CAME TO SAVE HER STARTED THAT FIRE?
THAT'S IMPOSSIBLE...

AFTER ALL, THE BODY OF THAT KUNOICHI WASN'T DISCOVERED AT THE SCENE OF THE FIRE, RIGHT?
TH... THAT'S TRUE, BUT...

THE SURVIVORS OF IGA MAY STILL BE OUT TO GET LORD NOBUNAGA.
SHFF
SHFF

PULL YOURSELF TOGETHER, RANMARU.
YES...!

AAAH... WHAT A RELIEF!!
I WAS ABLE TO SEND THE RED KONNYAKU TO LORD NOBUNAGA...
...SO THAT'S A LOAD OFF MY MIND.
WHAT IS IT?
YOU BOTH SEEM SO UNHAPPY...
OH, I KNOW.
DON'T WORRY ABOUT YOUR WEDDING.
I'LL HOST IT SOME-TIME THIS MONTH...
PLEASE WAIT!!

I'D LIKE TO...
...POSTPONE THE WEDDING FOR A WHILE.
HUH?
POST-PONE...?!
WE'VE GOT QUITE A LOT OF WORK TO DO SINCE WE WERE GONE...
RIGHT, USAGI?
UH-HUH...
I FELT RELIEVED.

I CAN'T MARRY YUKI FEELING THE WAY I DO...
YUKI...
DID HE POSTPONE THE WEDDING FOR ME...?
"I WANT YOU TO CONTINUE BEING THE USAGI WHO LOVES HANZO."
YUKI SAID THAT BECAUSE HE'S KIND...
It's so bright...

BUT IS IT RIGHT FOR ME TO TAKE ADVANTAGE OF HIS KINDNESS LIKE THIS ...?
USAGI?
ZUFF
ZUFF
I WAS TOLD SHE WENT PICKING HERBS...
SO WHERE COULD SHE BE...?
USAGI.

USAGI...?
ZZZ...
ZZZ...
ZZZ...
ZZZ...
HANZO...

OHH...
HNGH...
YOU WERE SLEEPING WELL.
YUKI?!
WHEN...
...DID I FALL ASLEEP...?
I HAVE TO TELL HIM...
I HAVE TO TELL HIM EVERY-THING...
YOU KNOW, USAGI...
YUKI, ACTUALLY...
HUH?
WHAT?
YOU GO AHEAD, YUKI...
NO, NO. YOU GO FIRST, USAGI.
UH...

I...
...DON'T KNOW HOW TO SAY THIS, BUT...
I WANT...
...TO CALL OFF OUR WEDDING...
I'M SORRY, YUKI!!
I'M...
I'M NOT SAYING THIS BECAUSE I DON'T LIKE YOU!!

IT'S JUST THAT IT DOESN'T FEEL RIGHT TO MARRY EACH OTHER...
...JUST BECAUSE WE CARE ABOUT ONE ANOTHER...
I'M REALLY SORRY!!
I'M REALLY, REALLY SORRY...
IT'S OKAY.
I CAME TO TELL YOU THAT WE SHOULD CALL OFF OUR WEDDING TOO.

YUKI ?!
I'M SORRY...
I HAVE MORE TO SAY.
CALM DOWN...
...AND LISTEN CAREFULLY.
BECAUSE...
...I REALLY DO LOVE YOU, USAGI.

WHEN YOU WERE CAPTURED BACK IN AZUCHI...
...YOU TOLD ME YOU DON'T REMEMBER HOW YOU ESCAPED, RIGHT?
UH-HUH...
BUT YOU SAVED ME, DIDN'T YOU, YUKI?
IT WASN'T ME.
JUST WHEN I LEFT THE LODGE TO LOOK FOR YOU...
...A NINJA CARRYING YOU APPEARED BEFORE ME AND LEFT YOU IN FRONT OF ME.
A NINJA ...?

HIS FACE WAS COVERED, SO I COULDN'T SEE IT CLEARLY...
BUT I THINK...
...IT MAY HAVE BEEN HANZO.

I CAN'T SAY FOR SURE NOW.
IT COULD HAVE BEEN A DIFFERENT NINJA WHO JUST LOOKED LIKE HIM.
BUT...
...I JUST COULDN'T KEEP IT A SECRET FROM YOU...
SQUEEZE
THANK YOU FOR TELLING ME ABOUT IT.
IT MUST HAVE BEEN HARD FOR YOU...
BUT THAT PERSON...
...PROBABLY ISN'T HANZO...

IF HANZO WAS ALIVE...
...HE'D DEFINITELY COME SEE ME!!
ZUFF
ZUFF
USAGI...
IF HANZO WERE ALIVE...
...I CAN'T IMAGINE HOW HAPPY I'D BE.
TRIP
AGH!

HUFF
HUFF
IF HANZO IS SOME-WHERE IN THIS WORLD...
HUFF
I WANT...
...TO SEE HANZO...

GOOD-NESS...
IT'S ALWAYS SO SUDDEN.
HUMPH...
YOU MUST BE PATIENT, MY LORD.
LORD IEYASU... I GOT THE HERBS YOU WANTED...
AH!
USAGI, CAN YOU HELP US WITH GETTING LORD IEYASU READY?
ARE YOU GOING SOME-WHERE?
I'VE BEEN SUMMONED TO AZUCHI CASTLE SUDDENLY...
OH, DEAR.
I SHOULDN'T BRING UP THAT PLACE IN FRONT OF YOU...

THAT'S ALL RIGHT.
AZUCHI...
IF HANZO REALLY WAS ALIVE...
...HE'D PROBABLY TRY TO GET REVENGE AGAINST NOBUNAGA...

WHAT'S WRONG?
WHY DID YOU STOP ALL OF A SUDDEN?
IF IT WERE HANZO ...
LORD IEYASU !!
YES?
I WANT TO GO TO AZUCHI WITH YOU!!
WHAT ?!

NO. NO, NO, NO.
YOU'RE A NINJA! HOW CAN WE TAKE YOU WITH US?!
BUT I'M AN HERBALIST NOW, SO...
LORD NOBUNAGA DESTROYED YOUR VILLAGE, SO WHY WOULD YOU WANT TO GO TO AZUCHI CASTLE?
UNLESS YOU'RE THINKING ABOUT REVENGE ...?!
ABSOLUTELY NOT!!
SOMETHING YOU WANT TO FIND OUT...?
THERE'S SOMETHING I WANT TO FIND OUT...
ARE YOU READY?
HUH?
!!

SHUP
I'M RANMARU MORI...
I'VE COME FROM AZUCHI TO ACCOMPANY YOU.
RAN-MARU!!

LET'S GO! LITTLE HANZO

MMM.

THANKS TO SUZUNE'S EDUCATIONAL GUIDANCE, HANZO'S PHYSICAL AND MENTAL STRENGTH GRADUALLY BECAME STRONG...

HMPH.

...

HOW-EVER ...

I WON'T LIE!!

LYING IS A PART OF A NINJA'S JOB.

IT'S WRONG TO LIE.

LOOK ...

THAT'S YOUR WEAK SPOT, HANZO.

HEH HEH HEH.

WHO'S THERE?!

FOOLISHLY HONEST NINJA ARE DOWNRIGHT MEANING-LESS, YOU KNOW.

CHATTER CHATTER

DO YOU KNOW WHAT IT MEANS TO BE FLEXIBLE?

HAN... ZOU...?!

LITTLE HANZOU SPOKE?! SO DOES THAT MEAN HE SUDDENLY GREW UP...? JOIN US NEXT TIME WHERE THE TRUTH WILL BE REVEALED!

Tail of the Moon
Chapter 93

"I'VE COME FROM AZUCHI TO ACCOMPANY YOU."
RAN-MARU?!
I CAN'T TAKE YOU TO AZUCHI WITH ME!
BUT...
THAT IS AN ORDER!!

LORD IEYASU.

LORD NOBUNAGA HAS REQUESTED THAT THE HERBALIST WHO MADE THE RED KONNYAKU YOU SENT HIM THE OTHER DAY...

...COME AS WELL.

WHAT?!

TH...THEN I'LL HAVE HER GET READY. PLEASE WAIT FOR A WHILE.

ALL RIGHT.

ARE YOU SURE I'M SUPPOSED TO WEAR SUCH A NICE KIMONO?!

YOU'RE GOING TO SEE LORD NOBUNAGA, SO YOU'VE GOT TO BE PROPERLY DRESSED.

THIS IS NERVE-WRACKING...

HUFF HUFF

USAGI...

TELL ME SOMETHING.

WHAT'S THE REASON YOU TO WANT TO GO TO AZUCHI FOR...?

WHAT?!
HANZO IS ALIVE?!
I DON'T KNOW FOR SURE.
BUT IF HE IS ALIVE, HE'LL PROBABLY GO AFTER NOBUNAGA FOR REVENGE, SO...
REVENGE ...?!
EXCUSE ME.
YUKI!!
USAGI...
YOU'RE GOING TO AZUCHI, RIGHT?

I WANT TO GO WITH YOU, BUT I'VE GOT MY WORK HERE TOO, SO...
IT'S OKAY, YUKI.
THANK YOU FOR EVERY-THING...
AND...
...I'M SORRY...
DON'T LOOK DOWN...
YOU LOOK THE BEST WHEN YOU'RE LOOKING UP...
...AND SMILING.
YUKI...

HANZOU...
PLEASE TAKE GOOD CARE OF HER.
I'LL DO EVERYTHING I CAN...
...BUT ONCE WE ENTER AZUCHI, THERE WILL BE A LIMIT AS TO HOW MUCH WE CAN DO TO PROTECT HER.
YOU STILL WANT TO COME WITH US THOUGH, RIGHT?
YES!!

EVEN THOUGH THE ROAD MAY BE ROUGH...
...I'M NOT AFRAID IF IT LEADS TO HANZO.
USAGI...
GOOD LUCK...

FIDGET
OW...
IT'S SO UNCOMFORT-ABLE RIDING IN THIS POSITION...
IF YOU'RE UNCOMFORT-ABLE, YOU CAN RIDE THE PALANQUIN INSTEAD.
I'M FINE.
ALL RIGHT, BUT PLEASE DON'T PUSH YOURSELF TOO MUCH.

CLIP
CLOP
IS HE UP TO SOMETHING AGAIN?
HUG
I HAVE TO STAY NEAR HANZOU AND THE OTHERS.
SIGH... I'M WORRIED...
MY LORD?
WHAT IF LORD NOBUNAGA FINDS OUT THAT USAGI USED TO BE A NINJA...?
MY LORD...
I USED TO BE A NINJA AS WELL...
THAT'S RIGHT!
I FORGOT ABOUT THAT.
HA HA

SHAA
THE WIND CHANGED...
HANZOU...
HAVE WE ARRIVED AT AZUCHI?
CLOP
CLOP
YEAH.
YOU NOTICED, HUH?
I CAN SMELL THE ENEMY.

NOBU-NAGA'S ...
...AZUCHI.
HUFF
HUFF
KAW
KAW
ALL THOSE LOVED ONES THAT NOBUNAGA KILLED...
SHUDDER
SHUDDER
WE CAN TURN BACK IF YOU WANT.
USAGI...
I'M FINE!
IT'S NOT JUST A PLACE WHERE MY ENEMIES ARE...

HANZO MIGHT BE HERE IN AZUCHI TOO.
下馬
DISMOUNT
AAAAGH!

WHAT'S WRONG, LORD IEYASU?!
I TWISTED MY BACK WHEN I GOT OFF THE HORSE...
OWW...
I'LL RUB SOME OINTMENT ON IT.
RUB
RUB
I GUESS I STILL NEED TO LOSE A BIT MORE WEIGHT...

LORD NOBUNAGA IS WATCHING SUMO RIGHT NOW...
...SO PLEASE FOLLOW ME.
ZUFF
ZUFF
PHEW.
ZUFF

NOKOTTA...
NOKOTTA!!
OOOH

HYAAAH
WHUMP
WH...!
...
WINNER...
UME-NO-WAKA!!
HMPH.
UME-NO-WAKA SURE IS STRONG, ISN'T HE!
CLAP
CLAP
OH.
CRUNCH
CRUNCH
LORD IEYASU...
LONG TIME NO SEE!
THANK YOU VERY MUCH FOR INVITING ME...
ZZT
ZZT
MMF.

MY LORD...
LORD IEYASU HAS ARRIVED...
HMM...
MFF...
NFF...
SILENCE
CRUNCH
CRUNCH
MY LORD ...?
WHO SHOULD I HAVE GO UP AGAINST HIM NEXT ...?

MITSUHIDE.
GO!
SHA
YES, SIR!
MITSUHIDE?
TMP
TMP
TRIP
FWUMP
OOF.
PULL YOURSELF TOGETHER ...
...MITSUHIDE!
I'M SORRY, MY LORD.
MITSUHIDE...
ARE HIS EYES GETTING BAD AGAIN?
HAKKEYOI...

...NOKOTTA!!
BOOSH
OOH.
MITSUHIDE IS PRETTY GOOD.
MITSU-HIDE...
HE WAS THE ONLY PERSON AMONG NOBUNAGA'S RETAINERS WHO WAS AGAINST THE ATTACK ON IGA...
UME-NO-WAKA.
IF YOU WIN THIS MATCH, I'LL GIVE MITSUHIDE'S SAKAMOTO CASTLE TO YOU.

?!
SAKAMOTO CASTLE...?!
GIVE HIM HIS CASTLE ...?!
WHAT A HORRIBLE ...!!
MURMUR
MURMUR
MITSUHIDE...
DO YOUR BEST...!
HUURGH...
LIFT
UNGH!
WOOSH
MITSUHIDE !!
MY LORD...
ARE YOU REALLY GOING TO GIVE SAKAMOTO CASTLE TO UME-NO-WAKA...?!
HA.

HUFF
HUFF
YOU FOOL...
PHEW
THAT'S NOT SOMETHING YOU JOKE ABOUT!!
HOW COULD HE?!
CRUNCH
I WAS ONLY JOKING.
IEYASU, YOU'RE NEXT!
Y... YES...
OW...
ZZZT
I'M SORRY, BUT LORD IEYASU HURT HIS BACK A MOMENT AGO, AND...
I'M FINE...
NGH.
ZZZT
YOU MUSTN'T DO IT...
HURRY UP!!

THEN...
...I'LL SUBSTITUTE FOR LORD IEYASU!!

HEY, THAT GIRL ...!!
MY LORD...
THAT GIRL IS...
YOU MUSTN'T ENTER THE RING!
WHY NOT?!
DO AS HE SAYS.
A NINJA?
...
FLIP
FLIP
CATCH
MY LORD, WHAT ARE YOU ...?
TOSS
TOSS
RAR
RAR
?
A walnut ?
SHAAA
WHY CAN'T I DO IT...?

WHONK
AGH!
OWWW!! WHAT WAS THAT...?
Mmft.
RAN-MARU...
WHAT KIND OF NINJA IS THAT?
HA HA HA HA HA
ER...
NINJA?!
LORD NOBUNAGA...
THIS GIRL IS FROM IGA, BUT SHE IS CURRENTLY WORKING AS MY HERBALIST...
IEYASU, I KNOW YOU'RE FOND OF THE NINJA...
...BUT COULDN'T YOU FIND SOMEONE BETTER THAN HER?!
HA HA HA HA HA

AHHH...
I'VE LAUGHED SO MUCH THAT I'M THIRSTY NOW...
WATER...
YOU COWARD.
I'VE HAD ENOUGH.
IT'S COWARDLY TO ATTACK SOMEONE FROM BEHIND AND THEN LAUGH ABOUT IT!!

IT'S DESPICABLE!
AND I REALLY, REALLY HATE YOU!!
STOP IT!!
I HA—
MMGH
YOU MUST APOLOGIZE!!
HOW DARE YOU TALK LIKE THAT...
...TO OUR LORD...?!

SHOVE
LET GO OF HER.
AH!
YOU...!!
USAGI...
SHA
YEEEAAGH!

LET'S GO! LITTLE HANZO

WERE YOU DECEIVING US WITH ALL YOUR BABY TALK THEN?!
AH. YOU FINALLY NOTICED THEN, HANZO?
HEH.

YOU'VE GOT TO TEACH ME HOW TO LIE LIKE YOU!!
WHAT, AND YOU THINK I'M GOING TO TEACH YOU FOR FREE?
HMM... WHAT SHALL I ASK FOR IN RETURN?

HAVE SOME OF THE HANZO FAMILY'S SPECIAL SYRUP!
YAY! ♪
NOW HURRY UP AND TEACH ME!!
WHAT ARE YOU DOING?
LICK
SHA

AAAAH ♡
HANZO... HOW DARE YOU SECRETLY EAT THAT ...?
HUH ?!
HANZO'S DAYS OF PHYSICAL TRAINING CONTINUE ...

WOW... I GUESS HANZOU WAS A BORN NINJA!! LITTLE HANZO, HANG IN THERE...!

Tail of the Moon
Chapter 94

STOP IT!!

RANMARU...
WHY DID YOU INTERRUPT ME?!
WHAT OBJECTION DO YOU HAVE IN TEACHING THIS RUDE KUNOICHI A LESSON?!
...
WELL...
KEE...

TMP
NGH.
GLOM
KEEE...
MOSUKE !!
WHY IS MOSUKE...?
THIS KUNOICHI TAMED MOSUKE WHEN SHE SNUCK INTO AZUCHI CASTLE LAST TIME!!
KEE...
I NEVER TAMED HIM!!

SADANARI.
PUT YOUR SWORD AWAY.
WHAT...?
SHUP
IT'S FINE.
IEYASU.
WE'LL BE HAVING YOUR FAVORITE TEMPURA FOR DINNER TODAY, SO LOOK FORWARD TO IT.
TMP
TMP
TH...
THANK YOU VERY MUCH.

YOU IDIOT!

YOU NEARLY GAVE ME A HEART ATTACK!!

JUST IMAGINE WHAT WOULD HAVE HAPPENED IF MOSUKE HADN'T APPEARED...!!

I'M SORRY...

KEE...

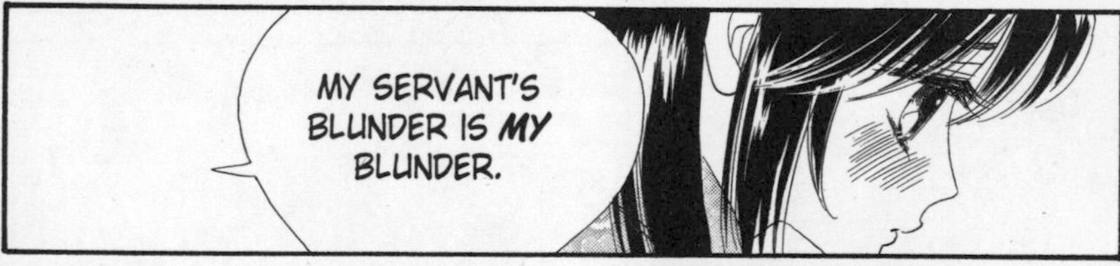

IF I AM TO BE PUNISHED...
...ALL OF MY RETAINERS AND THE PEOPLE OF MY LAND ARE GOING TO LOSE THEIR LIVELIHOOD.
OUR JOB IS TO PROTECT THE PEOPLE WHO SUPPORT OUR LAND.
YES...
DON'T EVER...
...TALK BACK TO LORD NOBUNAGA AGAIN.

THIS IS DELICIOUS !!

I JUST LOVE THE SCENT AND CRUNCHINESS!!

THE RED KONNYAKU YOU SENT ME WAS GOOD TOO.

THAT KONNYAKU ...

...WAS ACTUALLY MADE BY MY HERBALIST HERE...

TH-THUMP

HA HA.
SHE IS STILL YOUNG AND DOES NOT KNOW HER MANNERS...
...BUT SHE IS A VERY SKILLED HERBALIST.
BOW
GLARE
SO THAT GIRL IS YOUR HERBALIST ...

LET ME POUR YOU SOME SAKE.
THANK YOU.
EARLIER...
STOP IT!!
...I SURVIVED IN PART BECAUSE RANMARU STOPPED THE OTHERS.
DO YOU WANT SOME TOO?
I...I CAN'T DRINK, SO...
IS THAT SO?
I THOUGHT RANMARU WANTED TO KILL ME THOUGH...

THEN WHY...?
RAN...
...MARU...
THANK YOU...
...FOR HELPING ME OUT EARLIER...
I ONLY DID IT BECAUSE MOSUKE FAVORS YOU.
OH.
SO THAT'S WHY...

THE NEXT DAY

THIS CASTLE IS SO LARGE THAT I'D PROBABLY GET LOST IN IT.

TO TELL YOU THE TRUTH, I STILL GET LOST EVERY NOW AND THEN.

YOU DO?!
HAHA.
HEY...
WHAT'S THE MATTER?
I SMELL GUNPOWDER.
SNIFF
SNIFF
GUN-POWDER ?!

HOW CAN ANY-ONE BE USING GUNPOWDER HERE?! WE'VE GOT TO INVESTIGATE...
OH DEAR, OH DEAR...
THERE'S NO NEED FOR THAT.

BANG
FAK
SHAA
...
SO THE SCENT CAME FROM THESE RIFLES...
ZUFF
ZUFF
I'M SURPRISED YOU NOTICED THE SCENT OF THE GUNPOWDER EVEN THOUGH WE ARE UPWIND.
UM...

IEYASU.

WE'LL GO HUNTING TOMORROW WITH FALCONS AND THESE GUNS.

Y...YES.

SHWAA
SHWAA
SHWAA
SHWAA

BANG
FAK
SHUP

THE NEXT DAY
MY LORD...
HOW IS YOUR BACK TODAY?
I'M FINE NOW!
LORD IEYASU...
ARE YOU READY?
OH...
I'LL BE RIGHT THERE.
LET'S GO, USAGI.
WHAT?
I'M GOING TOO?
I CAN'T JUST LEAVE YOU HERE ALONE.
O... OKAY...
I WAS GOING TO LOOK FOR CLUES ABOUT HANZO WHILE EVERYBODY WAS AWAY...

IT'S ALREADY BEEN THREE DAYS SINCE WE CAME HERE...
...YET I STILL HAVEN'T DISCOVERED ANYTHING ABOUT HANZO.
HANZO MIGHT BE ALIVE.
AND IF HE IS, HE'D DEFINITELY COME TO GET REVENGE AGAINST NOBUNAGA.
THAT'S WHY I CAME HERE...
...BUT THINGS AREN'T GOING THE WAY I WANT THEM TO...

ZUFF
ZUFF
VISH
GO.
WHAT ARE YOU DOING, USAGI?
THERE'S AN INTERESTING HERB GROWING HERE...
...SO...

THE NUMBER OF GUARDS SURROUNDING HIM ARE JUST OVER-WHELMING.
IT'S NOT GOING TO BE EASY FOR ANY ASSASSIN TO GET NEAR HIM WITH SO MANY GUARDS...

HM?

I SMELL GUNPOWDER AGAIN...

IT MUST BE THE PILOT LIGHT I'M HOLDING.

SWISH

SWISH

IT'S NOT THAT SMELL.
IT'S SIMILAR BUT DIFFERENT.

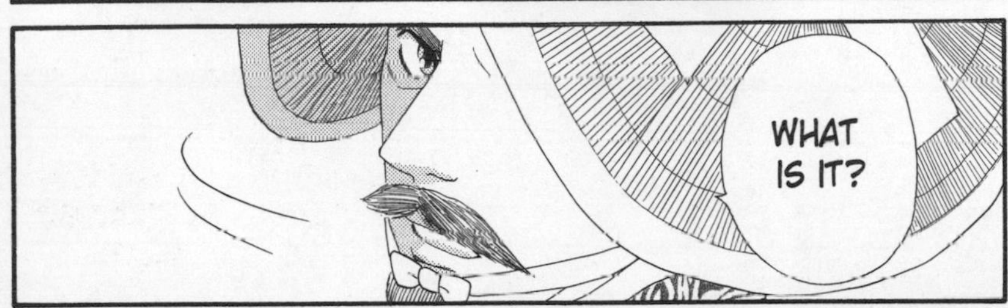

BANG

VISH
MY LORD !!
LORD NOBUNAGA !!

WHAT ARE YOU DOING?!
HURRY UP AND CAPTURE THAT ASSASSIN!!
YES, SIR.
IT CAME FROM THE FOREST!!
ASSASSIN...
COULD IT BE ...?
USAGI.
TREAT LORD NOBU-NAGA'S WOUND!!
Y...
...YES, SIR!!
RAR RAR
I...

FWOOM

I DON'T
BELIEVE
THIS...!!

WHOA, HANZOU REALLY IS SOMETHING... IS THAT WHY HANZO BECAME SUCH A SERIOUS PERSON? I CAN'T WAIT TO SEE WHAT HAPPENS NEXT...LOOK FORWARD TO THE NEXT ONE!

LET'S GO!
LITTLE HANZO
HANZO VISITED OKAZAKI TO LEARN ABOUT THE TECHNIQUES OF DECEPTION FROM HANZOU...
I'M HOOOME!
HANZO FROM IGA IS HERE TOO...
NICE TO MEET YOU. MY NAME IS HATTORI HANZO...
WELCOME HOME, HANZOU. ♡
I MISSED YOU, HANZOU...
AAAH...
MY DEAR HANZOU... ♡♡
WH... WHICH ONE IS YOUR MOTHER, HANZOU?
THESE ARE ALL MY GIRL-FRIENDS.
MMW
JE T'AIME♡
GIRL-FRIENDS ...?!
HANZO'S TRAINING CONTINUES ON...

I'M VERY SORRY.
WE'VE COMBED THE MOUNTAINS, BUT...
WHAT ?!
FIND THE ASSASSIN EVEN IF YOU HAVE TO BURN THE MOUNTAIN DOWN!!
I WON'T ALLOW YOU TO START A FIRE IN MY HUNTING GROUNDS.
Y...YES, SIR...
WE WON'T BURN IT, MY LORD.
HOW IS LORD NOBUNAGA'S WOUND?
IT'S NOT AS DEEP AS IT LOOKS.
I JUST NEED TO STERILIZE IT AND THEN PUT SOME OINTMENT ON IT.
THANK GOOD-NESS...
DO YOU THINK THE ASSASSIN IS AN IGA NINJA SURVIVOR?

ZUFF
ZUFF
ZUFF
ZUFF
WE DIDN'T FIND ANYBODY OVER HERE!!
DAMMIT...
WHERE DID THE ASSASSIN GO?!

LET'S GO!

LITTLE HANZO

PHEW

I'M ALL SWEATY ...

OH MY, LETS TAKE A BATH THEN.

YOU JOIN US TOO. ♡

TUG

HUH?

PARADISE~

HA HA HA HA HA HA

DO YOU WANT ME TO WASH YOUR BACK...?

NO, THANK YOU!!

SCRUB SCRUB

WO- MEN ...

FEARFUL CREATURES WITH ROUND BODIES THAT SHOW NO INDICATION OF THE DEVASTATING PUNCHES THEY WILL ATTACK YOU WITH...

HEY, HANZO!

LET'S PLAY.

HAHAHAHA

WHO KNOWS WHEN THEIR KINDLY FACES WILL TURN INTO THAT OF A DEMON...?

HANZO'S DISTRUST OF WOMEN CONTINUES ON...

I'M WORRIED ABOUT HANZO AND HANZOU... WHAT HAPPENS TO THEM AFTER THIS, AND WHY HAVE THEY TURNED OUT THE WAY THEY ARE NOW?! FIND OUT NEXT TIME!

THE RETURN OF...
A JAPANESE RHINOCEROS BEETLE WILL HAVE STOMACH TROUBLE IF YOU FEED IT WATERMELON.
HANZO'S TRIVIA

Tail of the Moon

Chapter 95

TREMBLE
TREMBLE
...
WHAT IF...?
WHAT IF IT WAS HANZO?
IT'S UNLIKELY BECAUSE A NINJA WOULD NOT USE A RIFLE THAT GIVES OFF A SCENT.

I SEE...
SO IT'S NOT HIM...?

I'M KIND OF HAPPY AND SAD AT THE SAME TIME...
AT ANY RATE, IT'S A GOOD THING WE HAVE USAGI TO HELP.
IEYASU.
YES?
GIVE ME THIS HERBALIST.

GIVE HER... ...TO YOU ...?
I'M ASKING YOU TO TURN HER OVER TO ME.
TUG
HUH?!
?!
SAY "NO," LORD IEYASU ...!!
YES, BUT...
B... BUT THIS HERBALIST USED TO BE A NINJA, SO...
EEEEK
SHE'S AN HERBALIST NOW, ISN'T SHE?
ARE YOU GOING TO GIVE HER TO ME OR NOT?

AS YOU WISH, LORD NOBUNAGA...
GOOD.
WHAAAAAAT?!

DO YOU HAVE A PROBLEM WITH THAT?
SHAKE
SHAKE

NO ONE CAN TALK BACK TO LORD NOBUNAGA...
LET'S RETURN TO AZUCHI CASTLE FOR NOW.

...!!
YOU'RE ALL GOING BACK TO OKAZAKI TOMORROW?!
THAT WAS THE PLAN FROM THE START.
NOOOOOO...
NOW, USAGI...
TUP
NO MATTER HOW UNREASONABLY YOU'RE TREATED, YOU MUST BEAR IT.
WHAT ...?!
FATHER ...
YOU'RE ONLY GOING TO SCARE HER IF YOU SAY SOMETHING LIKE THAT!
SHUDDER
SHUDDER
USAGI.
IN CASE OF AN EMERGENCY, THIS IS WHAT YOU NEED TO SAY...
...
GOT THAT?
SHOCK
DO I REALLY HAVE TO SAY THAT...?
WHAT DID YOU TELL HER?
JUST SOME WORDS OF ADVICE FOR HER TO GET ALONG HERE.

GLOOM
USAGI...
LORD NOBUNAGA IS A TEMPERAMENTAL MAN, BUT HE ISN'T A BAD PERSON.
IF YOU WORK FOR HIM WITH GOODWILL, HE WILL REPAY YOU WITH GOODWILL...
BUT...
...I'M SCARED...
USAGI...

HUG
YOU'RE MAKING IT TOO HARD FOR ME TO LET YOU GO WHEN YOU CRY LIKE THAT!!
URGH.
There, there...
WE'LL COME TO SEE YOU AS OFTEN AS WE CAN...
THE NEXT DAY
TAKE CARE OF YOURSELF.
IT'S A PROMISE ...!!
YOU HAVE TO COME BACK TO SEE ME SOON...!!
PSST
PSST
I HEARD SHE'S AN EX-NINJA...
MAYBE SHE'S GOT SOMETHING TO DO WITH THAT ASSASSIN FROM YESTERDAY...

I'VE GOT NOTHING TO DO WITH THAT!
I'M NOT SURE IF I'M GOING TO BE ABLE TO MAKE IT HERE...
DASH
MITSUHIDE ...
I'M GOING TO BE WORKING HERE STARTING TODAY...
MITSU-HIDE !!
SHA

HE IGNORED ME?!
MITSU...
DON'T.
TH-THUMP
RANMARU...
YOU'RE GOING TO MAKE THINGS DIFFICULT FOR HIM IF THE OTHERS FIND OUT HIS CONNECTION WITH YOU.
OH...
MAKE THINGS DIFFICULT FOR HIM ...?
PLEASE COME BY TO CHANGE LORD NOBUNAGA'S BANDAGE AFTER DINNER.
SO YOU WERE BACK IN SAKAMOTO WHILE I WAS GOING THOUGH SO MUCH TROUBLE...?
I'M VERY SORRY!!

THOK
I NEVER THOUGHT YOU WOULD BE IN DANGER...
VUP
...
IS SAKAMOTO MORE IMPORTANT TO YOU THAN ME?!

I'M SORRY, MY LORD.
MY EYE...
I'M PUTTING YOU ON PROBATION FOR A WHILE.
I DON'T WANT TO SEE YOUR FACE.

OW.
I'M SORRY.
IT HURTS, DOESN'T IT.
FUU...
FUU...
FUU...
HUH?
TUG
LORD NOBUNAGA?

!!
NGH...
NO...
I'M GOING TO MARK YOU AS MINE.

NO...
"NO MATTER HOW UNREASONABLY YOU'RE TREATED, YOU MUST BEAR IT."
"DON'T TALK BACK TO LORD NOBUNAGA."
BUT I CAN'T...
SOME-BODY ...
YOU MUSTN'T...
IF YOU MAKE LOVE TO ME...
...YOUR LIFE WILL BE IN DANGER...
WHAT DO YOU MEAN...?
I'M...
...A POISONOUS GIRL.

POISON-OUS?!
I DRANK POISONED MILK AS A BABY...
...AND HAVE WORN CLOTHING THAT HAS POISONOUS LEAVES WOVEN INTO THEM.
EVEN SO MUCH AS A KISS WOULD BE DEADLY ENOUGH TO KILL YOU.
SHA
SO I, MYSELF, AM "POISONOUS."

VERY WELL.
YOU CAN GO.
TMP
TMP
MY LORD...
DO YOU WANT ME TO CALL ONE OF YOUR CONCUBINES?

TMP
TMP
"LISTEN, USAGI..."
"IF ANYTHING SHOULD HAPPEN, SAY YOU ARE A POISONOUS GIRL TO GET AROUND IT."
ZWAK
HANZOU'S ADVICE REALLY WORKED...
HUFF
HUFF
BUT I NEVER THOUGHT I'D HAVE TO USE IT SO SOON...
I'M SCARED...

I...
I DON'T WANT TO STAY HERE.
EVEN IF I HAVE TO GO THROUGH ALL THIS HARDSHIP...
...THERE'S NO GUARANTEE THAT I'LL FIND ANYTHING ABOUT HANZO...

IF EVEN SO MUCH AS A KISS WOULD HAVE KILLED HIM...
...I WOULD HAVE BEEN DEAD SEVERAL TIMES BY NOW.
ZWAK
RANMARU...
WH...
WHAT...?

IF YOU DO ANYTHING TO ME...
...I'M GOING TO TELL LORD NOBUNAGA ABOUT IT.
I CAME TO SEE FOR MYSELF WHETHER YOU TRULY ARE A POISONOUS GIRL OR NOT...
THEN I CAN REPORT TO HIM ABOUT YOUR LIE.
STOP IT...

DASH
KEEE!!
PLEASE STOP THAT...!
MOSUKE...
KEE KEEE
TMP
TMP
WHAT'S GOING ON?!
IT'S NOTHING.
KEE KEE
RAN-MARU ...
WHAT ARE YOU DOING HERE?
Z-WAK
Z-WAK
KEE KEE
NOTHING, REALLY...

I MADE IT...
THANK YOU SO MUCH, MOSUKE...
KEE...
SHA
THAT'S...!
KEE?
THAT'S HANZO'S ARMBAND!
MOSUKE...
WHERE DID YOU GET THIS?!
WHERE DID YOU FIND IT...?
!!
A LETTER!!
RUSTLE
RUSTLE

"GO BACK TO... ...OKAZAKI"?
IT'S HANZO'S HAND-WRITING!!
SO HE REALLY IS ALIVE!!
NGH...
SNIFF...
RUSTLE
OKAZAKI. IF NOT,
CONSIDER YOU
IF...
...NOT...?

GO BACK TO OKAZAKI. IF NOT, I WILL CONSIDER YOU MY ENEMY AS WELL.
I'M...
...HANZO'S ENEMY?!

LET'S GO!

LITTLE HANZO

YOU WON'T BECOME A FINE NINJA UNLESS YOU LEARN TO GET OVER YOUR DISTRUST OF WOMEN, HANZO.

WH... WHAT AM I SUPPOSED TO DO?

MM

You've got a lot to learn...

YOU COMPLIMENT THEM EVERY MORNING AND EVERY NIGHT. ♪

SO I'M SUPPOSED TO COMPLIMENT THEM, HUH?

SCRIBBLE SCRIBBLE

YOU'RE BEAUTIFUL TODAY. YOU'RE THE BEST, MY SWEETHEART! ♡

SHA

HANZO.

I CAME TO PICK YOU UP.

OH, SUZUNE !!

YOU'RE AS BEAUTIFUL AS ALWAYS !!

ARE YOU MAKING FUN OF ME?

WHAT KIND OF PUNISHMENT DO YOU WANT TODAY?!

HUH ?

ER...

LIFT

HAN-ZO...

LITTLE HANZO TRIED HIS BEST TO UNDERSTAND FEMALE PSYCHOLOGY, BUT HE WAS NO MATCH FOR SUZUNE! GOOD LUCK, HANZO!

THE KANJI FOR "SMOKE SIGNAL" IS WRITTEN AS "狼煙" (WOLF SMOKE) BECAUSE THE SIGNAL IS CREATED THROUGH BURNING DRIED STRAW AND WOLF DUNG.
HANZO'S TRIVIA
Tail of the Moon
Chapter 96

"GO BACK TO OKAZAKI. IF NOT, I WILL CONSIDER YOU MY ENEMY AS WELL."
KEE...?
ZWAK
MOSUKE CAN'T LEAVE THE CASTLE ON HIS OWN.

KEE?
DOES THAT MEAN THAT HANZO WAS NEARBY?!
MAYBE HANZO...
...WAS LOOKING AT ME FROM SOMEWHERE ...?!
HUFF HUFF
I CAN'T FIND HIM...
RUSTLE
PLIP
GO BACK TO
I CAN'T GO BACK...

I CAME HERE TO SEE YOU, HANZO...
WHAT DO I HAVE TO DO TO SEE HIM...?
RUSTLE
...
SOMEONE'S THERE...
...BUT IT'S NOT RANMARU OR SOME OTHER ENEMY!!
HANZO?!
ZUFF
ZUFF
COME OUT IF YOU'RE THERE!!

WHERE...?
KEEEEEE!
ZUFF
ZUFF
YEAGH!
MOSUKE ?!
WHAT ARE YOU...?!
HUH?

WHAT'S THIS MONKEY'S PROBLEM?
LEMME GO!
WATARI?!
L...
LONG TIME NO SEE...
...HERBALIST.
YOU'RE KEEPING WATCH OVER ME?!
I THOUGHT THE ODA CLAN DIDN'T HAVE ANY NINJA WORKING FOR THEM...
I WAS PERSONALLY HIRED BY RANMARU.
RANMARU ...?

PLEASE DON'T TELL HIM THAT YOU NOTICED ME THOUGH!
I WON'T.

I STARTED WORKIN' TODAY WITH ORDERS TO KEEP AN EYE ON THE NEW HERBALIST...

...BUT I NEVER THOUGHT IT WOULD BE YOU!

BY THE WAY, IS MAMEZO AROUND HERE SOMEWHERE?
HE'S AT SAKAI RIGHT NOW.
OH...

I THOUGHT EVERYBODY WAS KILLED DURING THE ATTACK ON IGA...
...SO I WAS REAL GLAD TO FIND OUT THAT YOU GUYS ARE STILL ALIVE.
OH!
SHA

MOSUKE BROUGHT ME A NOTE FROM HANZO JUST A MOMENT AGO...
DO YOU KNOW ANYTHING ABOUT HANZO'S WHEREABOUTS, WATARI?

I DON'T.
I WAS TOLD THAT ALL THE HIGH-RANKING NINJA OF IGA WERE KILLED...
BUT I JUST GOT A LETTER FROM HANZO...!!
I REALLY DON'T KNOW ANYTHING ABOUT IT...
OH... SORRY...
SIGH...
...
DAD TOLD ME NOT TO TELL ANYBODY ABOUT THIS, BUT...
WHAT IS IT?!
THERE'S A RUMOR THAT THE WIFE OF OUR ASSISTANT LEADER...
...IS ACTUALLY A KUNOICHI FROM THE HATTORI CLAN.

HANZO'S OLDER SISTER!!
THAT'S RIGHT!
SHE MIGHT KNOW SOMETHING ABOUT THIS!!
HERBAL-IST...
FWOOSH
WHOA.
I'M GOING DOWN TO KOUGA.
HUH?!
WATARI, I NEED YOU TO HELP ME GET OUT OF AZUCHI CASTLE!!

SHWAAAAAA
...
WE'RE GONNA HAVE TO JUMP FROM ALL THE WAY UP HERE.
CAN YOU DO IT, HERBALIST?
YES!
I WON'T HOLD MYSELF BACK.

I'M SO HAPPY JUST KNOWING THAT HANZO IS ALIVE SOMEWHERE IN THIS WORLD.
WHUMP
AAAGH!
OWW...
ARE YOU OKAY?
I...
I'M FINE!

I CAN'T WAIT TO SEE HANZO.
HERBALIST, YOU'VE LOST WEIGHT. YOU'VE BE-COME REALLY PRETTY TOO...
HUH?
YOU WERE FATTER BEFORE AND HAD SHORT HAIR, BUT I THOUGHT I RECOGNIZED YOU.
Sesame dumplings...
I WASN'T POSITIVE UNTIL I GOT A GOOD LOOK AT YOUR FACE WHEN YOU CAME OUT TO THE GARDEN THOUGH.

WATARI.
DO YOU HAVE SOMETHING SHARP TO CUT WITH?
YEAH, RIGHT HERE...
LET ME BORROW IT!
SHUP
WH...?!
HEY...!
ZUFF
ZUFF ZUFF
HERB-ALIST?!

NOW I LOOK LIKE HOW I DID BEFORE, RIGHT?
UH-HUH...
BUT YOU LOOKED NICE WITH THE LONG HAIR...
Thanks for your blade.
I WANT HANZO TO KNOW IT'S ME THE MOMENT HE SEES ME.
HERB-ALIST...
YOU REALLY LIKE HANZO, DON'T YOU?

THAT'S RIGHT.
I LOVE HIM.
MY FEELINGS FOR HANZO HAVEN'T CHANGED SINCE THE DAY I MET HIM.
I CAN'T WAIT TO TELL HIM THAT.
NOW...
LET'S GO TO KOUGA!!

I JUST HOPE...

...SUZUNE KNOWS SOMETHING ABOUT...

WATARI!

DUCK!

HUH?

SHK SHK SHK SHK

YEEAGH!

WE... WE'RE NOT IN-TRUDERS...

I JUST CAME TO TALK TO MY SISTER-IN-LAW...

IS THAT YOU, USAGI?!

WHAT ARE YOU DOING HERE...?!
SUZUNE!!
YOU DIDN'T HAVE TO COME HERE IN THE MIDDLE OF THE NIGHT...
I WORK UNDER LORD NOBUNAGA NOW, SO I CAN ONLY SLIP OUT DURING THE NIGHT...
UNDER LORD NOBU-NAGA ?!
YES.
I WANTED TO SEE HANZO AGAIN, SO I—
HANZO ...?!
WHAT DO YOU MEAN BY THAT?
TAKE A LOOK AT THIS.
THIS IS HANZO'S HAND-WRITING !!
GO BACK TO OKA...

HE SENT ME THIS NOTE TODAY.

IT CAN'T BE...

I WAS TOLD THAT HANZO DIED IN THE ATTACK...

SO SUZUNE DOESN'T KNOW ANYTHING ABOUT IT EITHER ...?

BUT HE...

HE'S BEEN ALIVE ALL THIS TIME...!

I WENT TO AZUCHI TO LOOK FOR HANZO...
...BUT HE THINKS THAT I'M HIS ENEMY NOW...
WHAT ARE YOU TALKING ABOUT?!

HANZO DOESN'T WANT TO INVOLVE YOU IN HIS REVENGE AGAINST THE ODA CLAN.

HE WROTE THIS BECAUSE HE CARES FOR YOU, USAGI.

CARES...

...FOR ME...?

HE'S...
...THINKING ABOUT GETTING REVENGE ON HIS OWN.
THAT'S IMPOSSIBLE THOUGH!
WHETHER IT'S IMPOSSIBLE OR NOT ISN'T THE ISSUE. HE MUSTN'T DO IT.
REVENGE WILL ONLY BRING ABOUT MORE REVENGE. IT IS A FOOLISH ACT.
GREAT-GRANDPA SAID THE SAME THING TOO...
USAGI...
PLEASE HELP HANZO FOR ME...
YOU MUSTN'T LET HIM GET REVENGE.
HELP HIM BREAK FREE FROM THIS VICIOUS CYCLE OF SUFFERING!

HANZO IS...
...SUFFERING ALL ON HIS OWN...?
I CAN'T LET THAT HAPPEN!
OKAY!!
I WON'T LET HANZO GET HIS REVENGE!!
YOU CAN DO IT, USAGI. I HAVE FAITH IN YOU.
IF I FIND ANYTHING OUT ABOUT HANZO, I'LL HAVE WATARI CONTACT YOU.
THANK YOU!!

BE CAREFUL ON THE WAY HOME.
I WILL!

I WILL HELP HANZO.
I CAN FEEL MY STRENGTH GATHERING UP INSIDE ME!

HEEZE... HEEZE...
HEEZE...

HEEZE... HEEZE...
HERB-ALIST...?

LET'S...
...TAKE A BREAK...
GASP GASP
I'LL GO GET YOU SOME WATER.
TH... THANKS...

MAKING A TRIP TO AND FROM KOUGA IN ONE NIGHT IS TOUGH...
HEEZE... HEEZE...
WHAT BUSINESS DID YOU HAVE IN KOUGA?

AAAH!
RANMARU
!!
BOOSH
?
WHAT ARE YOU SCHEMING?
...

...
NOTHING, HM? WELL, I'LL MAKE YOU TALK ...
I WON'T TELL ANYONE, SO GO AHEAD AND TELL ME.
...EVEN IF I HAVE TO TORTURE YOU!
KRK
AAAH!
AAH!
SOMEBODY...
VISH
VISH
VISH
URGK!
VISH

AAGH!
WHAT THE...?!
SHUP
WHO...?
TCH...
...
KTCH

WHIP
HANZO!!

LET'S GO!

LITTLE HANZO

IF THIS GOES ON, HANZO'S GOING TO BECOME A WOMAN-HATER!!

Come with me...

I ALREADY HATE THEM...

Where are we going?

DASH

HI, HANZOU. HOW'VE YOU BEEN?

SHUP

MASTER TANBA...

I WANT YOU TO FIX HANZO'S DISLIKE OF WOMEN.

WHOA.

HOW ABOUT I LEND YOU MY GREAT-GRANDDAUGHTER USAGI UNTIL YOU OVERCOME THAT THEN?

WAARGH WAARGH

WH...?

WHOA! SHE STINKS !!

BLOOP BLOOP BLOOP

BUT YOU'RE JUST MAKING ME BABYSIT HER...

WAARGH WAARGH

GOOD LUCK!

AAARGH! STOP CRYING!!

PSHHHHH

Tail of the Moon
Chapter 97
IT'S NOT A DREAM...!!
HANZO'S TRIVIA
MELONS ARE ACTUALLY VEGETABLES.

GET OFF...
GRP
IS IT REALLY, REALLY YOU...?
...HANZO?!

IF YOU'VE BEEN ALIVE THIS WHOLE TIME...
...WHY DIDN'T YOU COME SEE ME?!
IT'S BEEN...
...SO DIFFICULT FOR ME.
I MISSED YOU SO MUCH...
GO BACK TO OKAZAKI.

DO IT!
WAIT!!
HANZO...
YOU'RE GOING AFTER NOBUNAGA, AREN'T YOU?!
IT DOESN'T CONCERN YOU.
OF COURSE IT DOES!
I DON'T WANT YOU TO DO ANYTHING DANGEROUS LIKE THAT!
SILENCE!

MY HEART DIED WHEN IGA WAS DESTROYED.
JUST...
...FORGET ABOUT ME.
NO...

I WON'T !!
DO AS I SAY...

DON'T SAY SUCH A HEART-BREAKING THING...
THERE HASN'T BEEN A DAY...
...WHERE I DON'T THINK ABOUT YOU, HANZO...

SO...
SHOVE
AGH...
WE CAN'T RETURN TO THOSE DAYS.
SHA
HANZO...

ZUFF
HANZO...
WAIT!!
ZUFF
DON'T GO!!
I WAS FINALLY ABLE TO SEE YOU...
ZSHMP
AAAH...
HUFF
HUFF
HE'S ALIVE...
HNGH...
UNGH...
SNIFF...

BUT I'VE LOST HIM AGAIN...
SNIFF...
NO...
NOOOOOO!

TMP
HERBALIST!
I'VE BEEN LOOKING EVERYWHERE FOR YOU...
WAAAGGHH

COLD-
HEARTED,
AREN'T
YOU.

THAT GIRL IS RELUCTANTLY WORKING UNDER NOBUNAGA JUST FOR THE CHANCE TO SEE YOU, YOU KNOW.

YOU SHOULD HAVE RUN OFF TO OKAZAKI WITH HER.
I CAN'T DO THAT.
I ALREADY MADE UP MY MIND TO BECOME THE DEVIL HIMSELF...

...TO AVENGE THOSE WHO DIED IN VAIN PROTECTING ME...
KRSHAA
MASTER HANZO, YOU MUST ESCAPE!!
WE'LL CUT THEM OFF HERE.
LET ME GO!
I'LL FIGHT TOO!
YOU MUSTN'T!!
BANG BANG
BANG
URGH!
BANG
BANG
ARGH...

HANG IN THERE!!
YOU CAN'T DIE!!
GRAB
!!
...!
THEY ALL WANT YOU TO LIVE.
YOU'VE GOT TO UNDER-STAND THAT.

IT WAS A MAJOR PAIN IN THE NECK...
...SAVING YOU BACK THERE.
I NEVER ASKED YOU TO SAVE ME.

YOU CAN THANK YOUR BRIDE-ELECT THEN. I SIMPLY HAD A DEBT TO PAY.

YOU'RE LUCKY TO STILL HAVE YOUR LIFE.

TAKE CARE OF IT.

NO ONE CAN GO AGAINST NOBUNAGA NOW ANYWAY.

SHUT UP!

I'LL KILL NOBUNAGA NO MATTER WHAT IT TAKES.

HERBALIST, WHAT AM I GONNA DO...?
RANMARU KNOWS I'VE BEEN TALKING TO YOU, SO HE'S GOING TO BE ANGRY...
JUST STAY BY MY SIDE, WATARI.
I WON'T LET RANMARU LAY A FINGER ON YOU.
HERBAL-IST...
ZZZ...

"MY HEART DIED WHEN IGA WAS DESTROYED."
HANZO ISN'T THE KIND OF PERSON WHO'D EASILY CHANGE HIS MIND.
HOW CAN I STOP HANZO FROM GETTING HIS REVENGE ...?
AND HOW CAN I GET HANZO BACK?

HOW CAN I...?
BUMP
AGH!
WHOA!
PLEASE BE CAREFUL.
I'M SORRY...
IS THAT LORD NOBUNAGA'S BREAKFAST?
YES...
THEN I'LL TAKE IT TO HIM.
BUT THIS IS MY JOB...
I'VE BEEN ORDERED TO BECOME HIS FOOD TASTER STARTING TODAY.
IF YOU DON'T BELIEVE ME, YOU CAN ASK LORD NOBUNAGA HIMSELF.
OH ?!

SCAN SCAN
SHUP
THEN... PLEASE BE CAREFUL WITH IT.
I WILL!
I'LL KILL NOBUNAGA MYSELF!!

KRK
ONCE NOBUNAGA IS DEAD, HANZO WON'T BE ABLE TO GET HIS REVENGE.
THEN I'LL BE ABLE TO GET HANZO BACK!!
!
WHY ARE YOU...?

YOUR PAGE ASKED ME TO BRING THIS TO YOU...

SADA-NARI.

TASTE IT.

YES, MY LORD.

I CAN'T LET ANYBODY ELSE EAT IT!!

I'LL TASTE IT FOR YOU THEN.

I CAN DISTINGUISH EVEN THE SLIGHTEST OF POISONS, YOU SEE.

FINE...

BUT DON'T PUT YOUR MOUTH ON THE BOWL.

Y... YES, SIR.

SHP

MNCH

MNCH

GULP

THERE'S NOTHING WRONG WITH IT.

THE POISON HAS NO EFFECT ON ME...

...BUT IT'S STRONG ENOUGH FOR AN ORDINARY PERSON TO DIE FROM IT.

IT'S NOT INSTANTANEOUS...

...SO IT WILL TAKE A WHILE FOR THE POISON TO TAKE EFFECT.

I'LL BE FINE AS LONG AS I GET OUT OF HERE BEFORE THE POISON STARTS WORKING.

AH.

WHERE'S RANMARU?

I HAVEN'T SEEN HIM SINCE THE MORNING...

TH-THUMP TH-THUMP

FOR GOD'S SAKE...
GOOD-BYE, ODA NOBUNAGA.

LET'S GO!

LITTLE HANZO

TO GET OVER HIS DISLIKE OF WOMEN, HANZO DECIDED TO TAKE CARE OF BABY USAGI. ♪

WAAAARGH

WAAARGH

SHUT UP AND KEEP STILL! I'M TRYING TO WASH ALL THE DIRT OFF YOU!!

YOU'RE CLEAN AT LAST.

NOW THAT I GOT A GOOD LOOK AT YOU, YOU'RE ACTUALLY A VERY CUTE BABY.

Aaah...

NEAT FANATIC

I GUESS I'VE GOT SOME FATHERLY LOVE INSIDE ME...

There, there.

VEEN ♡

PAT PAT

FWASH

BURRP

USAGI DRANK A LOT OF MILK JUST A WHILE AGO...

MGH!

HANZO SAID I WAS CUTE! ♡ I MUST HAVE BEEN THE ONE WHO ROUSED THE FATHERLY LOVE INSIDE HIM...!

HANZO'S TRIVIA
APRICOT JAM WAS USED INSIDE THE WORLD'S FIRST JAM-FILLED BUN.
Tail of the Moon
Chapter 98

GOODBYE...

NO, I CAN'T ...!!
LORD NOBU-NAGA...
SHFF
SHFF
I'M SORRY I'M LATE!!
RANMARU...
I'M SORRY FOR BEING LATE. I OVER-SLEPT.
HE'S LYING.
AAGH
RANMARU WAS INJURED WHEN HANZO THREW THAT NINJA STAR AT HIM...
IT'S NOT LIKE YOU TO OVERSLEEP, RANMARU.

OVER-SLEEPING IS SOMETHING THAT THOSE WHO ARE NOT SERIOUS DO!
SHATTER
MY LORD...
YOUR BREAK-FAST...
SHFF
SHFF
I DON'T WANT IT!!
IT WORKED OUT FOR THE BEST IN THE END...

I... CAN'T DO IT AFTER ALL...
NGH
WHO COULD IT BE THIS LATE AT NIGHT...?
NOBU-NAGA ?!

I HEARD LORD NOBUNAGA NEVER SLEEPS.
POP
WATARI...
You startled me...
NEVER SLEEPS...?
HE STAYS AWAKE THINKING ABOUT THE NEXT BATTLE AND ABOUT POLITICS...
WELL, THAT'S WHAT DAD TOLD ME.
HMM...
EXCUSE ME...

WOULD YOU LIKE SOME TEA?
I'LL HAVE SOME.
MY LORD?
HERE.
SIP
AH.
IT'S GOOD TEA.
THANK YOU VERY MUCH.
...
FWUMP
?!
ZZZ...
RANMARU ...
LEND ME YOUR LAP.
YES, SIR.

ZZZ...
ZZZ...
USAGI!
WHAT DID YOU PUT IN THAT TEA?!
IT'S NOTHING BAD...
JUST A LITTLE SLEEPING POWDER...

SLEEPING POWDER?!
I WAS TOLD THAT LORD NOBUNAGA HARDLY EVER SLEEPS...
...SO I THOUGHT HE HAD INSOMNIA.
INSOMNIA IS AN ILLNESS WHERE YOU CAN'T SLEEP EVEN IF YOU WANTED TO, SO I THOUGHT I'D...
LORD NOBUNAGA...

...IS AN EXTREMELY TOLERANT MAN. HE DOESN'T CARE ABOUT YOUR SOCIAL STATUS OR YOUR PAST AS LONG AS YOU HAVE THE SKILLS TO DO WHAT IT TAKES.
HE WOULD EVEN HIRE MILITARY COMMANDERS WHO USED TO BE HIS ENEMY...
HIS PAST ENEMIES...
HIS NEW ENEMIES...
HE IS PUTTING HIS HEART AND SOUL INTO HIS WORK SO THAT HE CAN UNITE EVERYONE AS ONE.
THERE ARE THOSE WHO FEAR HIM AND THINK OF HIM AS BEING A DEMON, A FIEND...
BUT TO ME...
...LORD NOBUNAGA IS THE GOD OF THIS NEW WORLD.

NEW WORLD ...?
MM...
SHUP
DON'T YOU WANT TO SLEEP A LITTLE LONGER?
NO... I FEEL A LOT BETTER.
WHAT ...
YOU'RE STILL HERE?
P...
PLEASE EXCUSE ME.
SHFF
HE'S STILL SCARY.
SHFF
THE TEA WAS GOOD.
MAKE ME SOME AGAIN SOME-TIME.

STRANGE...
THANK YOU VERY MUCH FOR SAYING SO.
WHEN I WAS LOOKING AT HIM FROM THE OUTSIDE, NOBUNAGA WAS AN ENEMY WHOM I HATED.
BUT NOW THAT I'VE SEEN HIM UP CLOSE...
...HE SEEMS VERY DIFFERENT.

A FEW DAYS LATER

LORD IEYASU IS COMING?!

KEE.

MITSUHIDE WILL BE THE HOST. HE SEEMS BUSY, SO WHY DON'T YOU HELP HIM?

ALL RIGHT!
I CAN TALK TO LORD IEYASU ABOUT HANZO.

LORD IEYASU IS ON A DIET PRETTY MUCH THROUGHOUT THE YEAR, SO I DON'T THINK IT'S A GOOD IDEA TO HAVE TEMPURA.

THEN WHAT ABOUT GRILLED SEA BREAM WITH SALT?
LORD IEYASU LOVES SEA BREAM, SO THAT'S PERFECT!
SEA BREAM IT IS...
GLANCE
MITSU-HIDE...
HOW ARE YOUR EYES DOING?
WHISPER
I'M FINE.
PHEW
MITSUHIDE.
HIROKO !!
THIS IS MY WIFE, HIROKO...
I CAME TO HELP YOU.
ARE YOU USAGI, THE HERBALIST, BY CHANCE?
OH...
YES, I AM.

THE MEDICINE YOU MADE FOR MY HUSBAND...

YOU MUSTN'T TALK ABOUT THAT HERE.

OH...

I'M SORRY.

AT ANY RATE, I'M GLAD YOU CAME TO HELP ME.

I'LL GO AND ORDER THE SEA BREAM RIGHT AWAY!

GOOD LUCK.

MITSUHIDE'S REALLY WORKING HARD, ISN'T HE!

HE MUST REALLY WANT THIS FEAST TO BE SUCCESSFUL SINCE IT'S HIS FIRST LARGE ASSIGNMENT AFTER HIS SUSPENSION.

HIROKO...

YOU MUST KNOW ABOUT IT IF YOU WORK HERE, DON'T YOU?

HOW LORD NOBUNAGA IS DISPLEASED WITH MY HUSBAND...

WELL...
I WANTED TO BE OF SOME HELP TO HIM SOME-HOW.
I JUST COULDN'T STAY PUT AT SAKAMOTO CASTLE.
I'VE HEARD THAT MITSUHIDE DOESN'T HAVE ANY CONCUBINES AND THAT HE'S FULLY DEVOTED TO HIS WIFE, HIROKO.
THEY REALLY ARE A FINE COUPLE, AREN'T THEY.
HOW NICE.
LET'S WORK HARD TOGETHER SO THAT HIS JOB WILL BE A SUCCESSFUL ONE.
I WISH HANZO AND I COULD BE LIKE THEM...

THREE DAYS LATER
USAGI!
YOU LOOK GREAT!!
LORD IEYASU...
WELCOME, IEYASU.
I'VE ASKED MITSUHIDE TO HAVE TONIGHT'S FEAST PREPARED.
BOW
BOW BOW
AH.
THANK YOU VERY MUCH.
I HELPED WITH THE FEAST TOO...
EXCELLENT, USAGI.
WHAT'S THIS?
IT STINKS!
HM?
THERE DOES SEEM TO BE A FISHY SMELL...

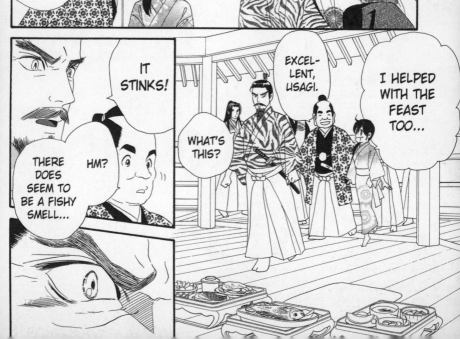

WHY WAS A *RAW* SEA BREAM PLACED HERE?!
THAT'S IM-POSSIBLE...
WHUP
MITSUHIDE !!
I'M SORRY, MY LORD!!

KLATTER
CAN'T YOU EVEN GET A SIMPLE FEAST READY?!
THIS HAS TO BE A MISTAKE.
MITSUHIDE *DID* GET THE FEAST PROPERLY READY...
NO!!
IT IS MY MISTAKE!!
MITSU-HIDE...
YOU'RE USELESS!
IEYASU...
I'LL HAVE SOMEONE ELSE PREPARE A FEAST RIGHT AWAY.
OH NO, DON'T WORRY ABOUT IT...

WIPE
WIPE
CHAK
NGH...
SNIFF...
YOU NEEDN'T CRY, USAGI.
BUT...
YOU...
YOU *DID* HAVE THE FEAST READY.
BUT HE WOULDN'T EVEN LISTEN...
HOW COULD HE...?
IT'S OVER AND DONE WITH.
WHY DIDN'T YOU ARGUE WITH HIM?!

YOU ALWAYS LET HIM SAY WHAT HE WANTS...
LORD NOBUNAGA DEPENDS ON ME.
IF YOU THINK ABOUT IT THAT WAY, THERE'S NOTHING TO GET ANGRY ABOUT, RIGHT?

TO NOT GET ANGRY...
THE SPIRIT OF FORGIVENESS...
"REVENGE WILL ONLY BRING ABOUT MORE REVENGE. IT IS A FOOLISH ACT."
"WE'RE GOING TO SIT BACK AND ENJOY WHAT KIND OF COUNTRY NOBUNAGA'S GOING TO CREATE, RIGHT?"

WAAARGH!
WHAT IS IT?!
I...
I FINALLY UNDERSTAND...
REVENGE WON'T SOLVE ANYTHING.
MITSUHIDE...
THANK YOU...
THAT'S WHY I HAVE TO STOP HANZO...
...FOR HIS OWN SAKE!!

OMI, SAKAMOTO CASTLE
MOTHER...
IT'S NOT GOOD FOR YOUR HEALTH TO BE EXPOSED TO THE NIGHT WIND.
I'M PRAYING.
I PRAY...
...THAT YOUR FATHER'S WORK WILL BE SUCCESS-FUL...

AND...
...I HOPE HE WILL BE SAFE AND SOUND IN AZUCHI...
I HAVE A MESSAGE FROM LORD NOBUNAGA.
MAY I READ IT TO YOU HERE?
SURE...
"THE LANDS OF OMI AND TANBA WHICH MITSUHIDE CURRENTLY HOLDS WILL BE TAKEN..."
"...AND HIS NEW DOMAIN WILL BE IZUMO OF THE SANIN AREA."
TAKEN...?
HE'S DEPRIVING MITSUHIDE OF HIS LAND?!
...

BUT...
IZUMO BELONGS TO THE ENEMY...!
THAT'S WHY HE SAID, "DESTROY THE MOURI CLAN AND SEIZE IT..."
BUT THAT'S ...!!
PLEASE LEAVE SAKAMOTO CASTLE AS SOON AS POSSIBLE.
TO BE CONTINUED...

The ways of the ninja are mysterious indeed, so here is a glossary of terms to help you navigate the intricacies of their world.

Page 2: **Ranmaru Mori**
Ranmaru Mori is one of Oda Nobunaga's most famous vassals. He became Nobunaga's attendant at a young age and was recognized for his talent and loyalty.

Page 8, panel 1: **Azuchi Castle**
Azuchi Castle was one of Oda Nobunaga's main castles. It is located on the shores of Lake Biwa in Shiga prefecture. The castle's strategic location enabled Nobunaga to manage his foes more easily, namely the Uesugi clan to the north and the Mouri clan to the west.

Page 10, panel 1: **Konnyaku**
Konnyaku is a traditional Japanese jelly-like health food made from the starch of the "devil's tongue" plant (a relative of the sweet potato).

Page 41, panel 5: **Nokotta**
Along with "hakkeyoi," "nokotta" is an expression used by the referee in sumo to keep the wrestlers going.

Page 44, panel 1: **Mitsuhide Akechi**
Mitsuhide Akechi became one of Oda Nobunaga's retainers after Nobunaga's conquest of Mino province (now Gifu prefecture) in 1566. He is known to have been more of an intellectual and a pacifier than a warrior.

Page 2: **Oda Nobunaga**
Oda Nobunaga lived from 1534 to 1582, and came close to unifying Japan. He is probably one of the most famous Japanese warlords. He was the first warlord to successfully incorporate the gun in battle and is notorious for his ruthlessness.

Page 2: **Iga**
Iga is a region on the island of Honshu and also the name of the famous ninja clan that originated there. Another area famous for its ninja is Kouga, in the Shiga prefecture on Honshu. Many books claim that these two ninja clans were mortal enemies, but in reality inter-ninja relations were not as bad as stories might suggest.

Page 2: **Tokugawa Ieyasu**
Tokugawa Ieyasu (1543-1616) was the first Shogun of the Tokugawa Shogunate. He made a small fishing village named Edo the center of his activities. Edo thrived and became a huge town, and was later renamed Tokyo, the present capital.

Page 2: **Okazaki Castle**
Okazaki Castle is in the city of Okazaki in Aichi prefecture. This castle was home to various leaders throughout history, including Tokugawa Ieyasu. Though demolished in 1873, the castle was reconstructed in 1959.

Page 92, panel 6: Sakamoto
Sakamoto is a small village in Shiga prefecture (once known as Omi province). In 1571, Mitsuhide Akechi was awarded the Sakamoto estate for serving Oda Nobunaga.

Page 115, panel 4: Sakai
Sakai is a city in Osaka prefecture that is one of the largest and most important seaports in Japan. Once known for samurai swords, Sakai is now famous for quality kitchen knives and other cutlery.

Page 116, panel 5: Kunoichi
A term often used for female ninja. The word is spelled くノ一, and when combined, the letters form the kanji for woman, 女。

Nobunaga finally makes his appearance. When drawing people who actually existed, you end up creating something like a history tutorial manga if you're not careful. Since this story is fiction, I've added my own flavor of personalities to the characters to make it more dramatic.

–Rinko Ueda

Rinko Ueda is from Nara prefecture. She enjoys listening to the radio, drama CDs, and Rakugo comedy performances. Her works include *Ryo*, a series based on the legend of Gojo Bridge; *Home*, a story about love crossing national boundaries; and *Tail of the Moon (Tsuki no Shippo)*, a romantic ninja comedy.

TAIL OF THE MOON

Vol. 14

The Shojo Beat Manga Edition

STORY & ART BY

RINKO UEDA

Translation & Adaptation/Tetsuichiro Miyaki
Touch-up Art & Lettering/Mark McMurray
Design/Izumi Hirayama
Editor/Amy Yu

Editor in Chief, Books/Alvin Lu
Editor in Chief, Magazines/Marc Weidenbaum
VP, Publishing Licensing/Rika Inouye
VP, Sales and Product Marketing/Gonzalo Ferreyra
VP, Creative/Linda Espinosa
Publisher/Hyoe Narita

Printed in Canada

Published by VIZ Media, LLC
P.O. Box 77064
San Francisco, CA 94107

Shojo Beat Manga Edition
10 9 8 7 6 5 4 3 2 1
First printing, December 2008

www.viz.com

store.viz.com

PARENTAL ADVISORY

TAIL OF THE MOON is rated T+ for Older Teen and is recommended for ages 16 and up. This volume contains brief nudity and ninja violence.

ratings.viz.com